ENCYCLOPÆDIA

Britannica DISCOVER AMERICA

Oregon

The Beaver State

ENCYCLOPÆDIA
Britannica®

CHICAGO LONDON NEW DELHI PARIS SEOUL SYDNEY TAIPEI TOKYO

EB STAFF ACKNOWLEDGEMENTS

Editors
Linda Berris
Mark Domke
Anthony L. Green
James Hennelly
William L. Hosch
Gene O. Larson
Michael I. Levy
Robert M. Lewis
Tom Michael
Colin Murphy
Sarah Forbes Orwig
Amy Tikkanen
Jeffrey Wallenfeldt

Copy Editors
Michael Anderson
Andrea R. Field
Lorraine Murray

Cover Design and Art
Nancy Donohue Canfield
Kurt Heintz
Steven C. Lencioni
Kristine A. Strom

WEIGL STAFF ACKNOWLEDGEMENTS

Editor
Michael Lowry

Copy Editor
Diana Marshall

Designers
Warren Clark
Terry Paulhus

Photo Researcher
Angela Lowen

This edition published 2005 by Encyclopædia Britannica, Inc.
310 South Michigan Avenue
Chicago, IL 60604

International Standard Book Number: 1-59339-183-8

Library of Congress Control Number: 2004112601

ENCYCLOPÆDIA Britannica: DISCOVER AMERICA
Volume 37: Oregon 2005

Britannica.com may be accessed on the Internet at
http://www.britannica.com.

Printed in the United States of America
1 2 3 4 5 6 7 8 9 0 09 08 07 06 05 04

Photograph Credits

Every reasonable effort has been made to trace ownership and to obtain permission to reprint copyright material. The publishers would be pleased to have any errors or omissions brought to their attention so that they may be corrected in subsequent printings.

Cover: Columbia River Gorge, Oregon, © **Royalty-Free/CORBIS**; **Corbis Corporation:** pages 3B, 13T, 15T, 15B, 26B; **Corel Corporation:** pages 3T, 3M, 5BL, 5T, 8T, 8B, 9T, 9B, 10T, 10B, 11T, 11B, 13B, 14T, 14B, 19B, 21T, 26T, 28T, 29B; **David Falconer:** pages 4T, 4B, 6, 7T, 7B, 12T, 12B, 20BL, 20BR, 22T; **Donna Ikenberry:** pages 16B, 20T; **Bruce Leighty:** page 21B; **Oregon Historical Society:** pages 16T, 17T, 17B, 18T, 18B, 19T; **PhotoDisc Corporation:** pages 27T, 27B, 28R; **Photofest:** pages 24T, 25T, 25B; **Bob Pool:** pages 22B, 23T, 23BR, 24B.

CONTENTS

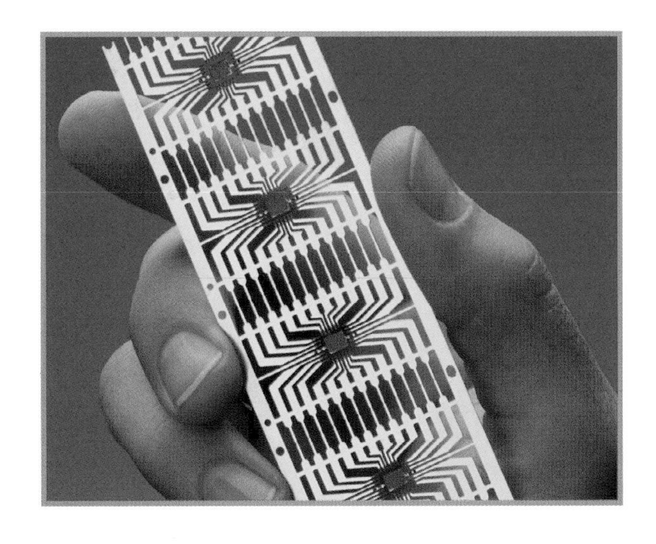

Reaching heights of over 10,000 feet, Oregon's mountains are an impressive sight.

INTRODUCTION

Located in the beautiful Pacific Northwest, Oregon has been attracting visitors for centuries. In the mid-1800s some 300,000 to 500,000 pioneers followed the Oregon Trail westward from Missouri, many of them taking it all the way to Oregon's fertile Willamette Valley. These early settlers were attracted to the state's abundant supply of furs, its fertile land, and its rich forests. Their journey has been called the Great **Migration**.

No one knows for sure where the name Oregon came from. It is believed that early French settlers used the name *ouragan*, meaning "hurricane," for the mighty Columbia River. Today Oregon's stunning combination of mountains, forest, and coastline has led many to refer to the state as the Pacific Wonderland.

Quick Facts

Salem was established as the territorial capital of Oregon in 1851.

Oregon's birthday is on St. Valentine's Day, Feb. 14, 1859.

Oregon is nicknamed the Beaver State. The beaver was an important source of income for early trappers in Oregon.

The Pacific Northwest is a region in the northwestern United States along the Pacific coast. It includes the states of Washington and Oregon as well as parts of northern California, western Canada, and southern Alaska.

Portland's Japanese Garden is considered to be one of the most beautiful gardens of its kind outside of Japan.

Oregon was the first state to complete its part of the interstate freeway system in 1966.

Oregon's western border follows the Pacific coast. The state is bordered by Washington to the north, Idaho to the east, and California and Nevada to the south. The Columbia River forms most of the border dividing Oregon from Washington, and the Snake River forms a large section of the border dividing Oregon from Idaho.

Oregon's road network is immense. The state's area of more than 97,000 square miles is crossed by well-developed roads and highways. Running the length of the Oregon coast, the Pacific Coast Scenic Byway offers spectacular views of the picturesque coastline.

Portland International Airport is the largest of seven commercial-passenger airports in Oregon. The airline industry is an important part of Oregon's economy as Portland and other airports serve as gateways to Asia.

Quick Facts

Nine historic lighthouses dot the Oregon coastline, from Tillamook Rock Lighthouse in the north to Cape Blanco Lighthouse in the south.

Oregon has the only state flag with a different image on each side. On the front, the words State of Oregon are written in gold across the top of the flag. On the back, a gold beaver is pictured on a field of navy blue.

Front side of Oregon flag

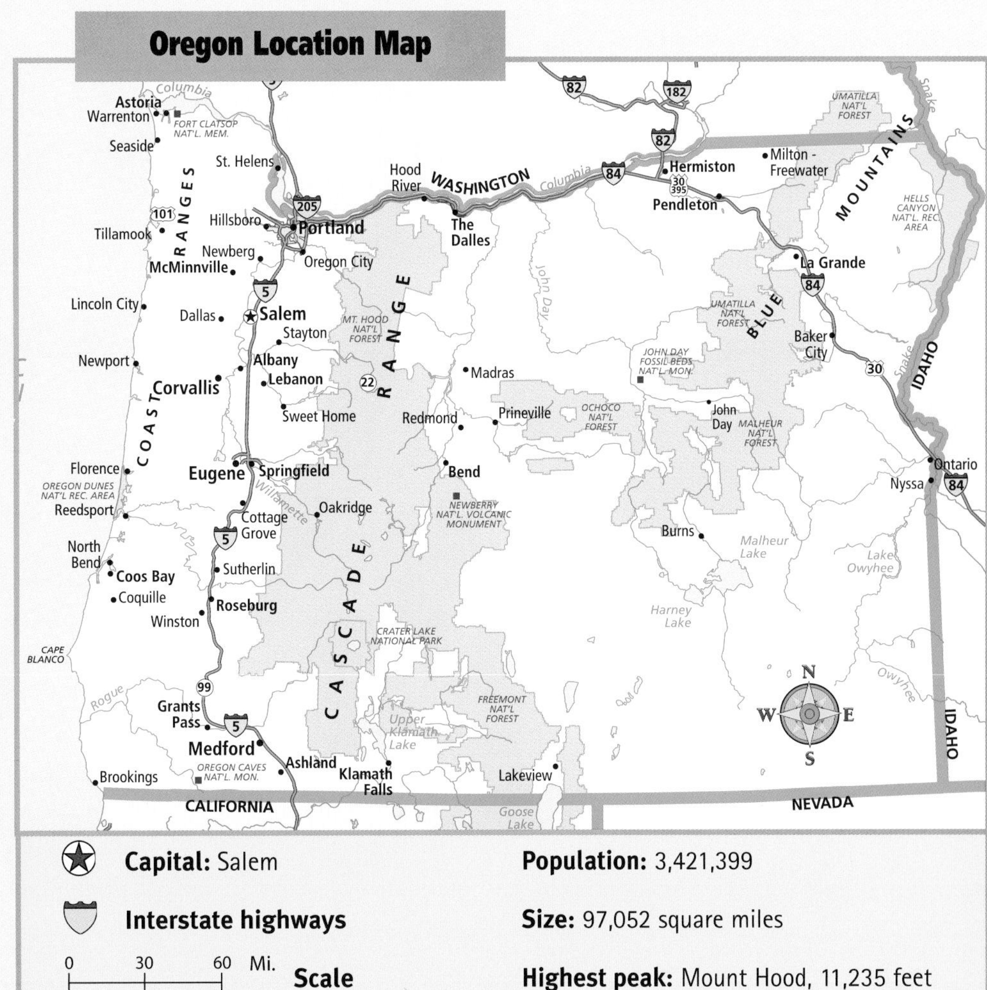

Spanish explorers may have first sailed the coastal waters off Oregon as early as 1543. Eventually many European nations were drawn to the area for its wealth of fur-bearing animals and their valuable pelts. Following the **Louisiana Purchase** of 1803, U.S. President Thomas Jefferson sent Meriwether Lewis and William Clark to explore the North American continent west of the Mississippi River. Their successful expedition to the Oregon coast encouraged trappers and settlers to journey to Oregon throughout the 1800s.

With the European settlers came European diseases, which resulted in the deaths of many Native Americans. Competition between the settlers and the Native Americans over valuable land and natural resources often developed into violent conflicts. In 1823 the U.S. Supreme Court ruled that because the Native Americans were "wanderers" they did not own their land. This ruling provided a convenient justification for taking the Native Americans' homelands away from them. In 1859 Oregon became the 33rd state of the United States, and the logging and farming industries fueled the new economy.

The Portlandia statue, in Portland, is the second largest hammered-copper statue in the country.

QUICK FACTS

Douglas Engelbart, who is responsible for inventing the computer mouse, was born near Portland.

The state gemstone is the sunstone, a brightly colored transparent gem in the feldspar family.

Oregon has more than 1,700 lakes.

One environmental protection program, the Oregon Plan, was developed to restore salmon and trout populations in the state.

During the second half of the 20th century some of Oregon's traditional industries, such as forestry and fishing, were threatened. Overfishing of salmon and aggressive logging of national forests led to a severe decline of these resources. Environmental protection laws were created to protect the state's natural resources. While the traditional industries were forced to adapt to these challenges, new high-technology industries, such as electronics, developed and strengthened the state's economy.

Oregon is a haven for outdoor recreation. The mountains and coastline provide a wealth of opportunity for activities such as swimming, skiing, boating, hunting, and fishing. The Columbia River Gorge in northern Oregon has become one of the most popular places in the world to windsurf. Today Oregon's friendly population and diversified economy attract people from all over the world.

Quick Facts

In 1996 Oregon became the first U.S. state to elect a senator entirely by mail-in ballot.

Oregon has one of the highest minimum wages in the United States.

At 620 feet, Multnomah Falls is one of the highest waterfalls in the United States.

Oregon's motto is *Alis Volat Propiis*, a Latin phrase meaning "She Flies with Her Own Wings."

The state song is "Oregon, My Oregon," by J.A. Buchanan and Henry B. Murtagh.

Oregon has nearly 300 miles of coastline.

LAND AND CLIMATE

Oregon has a varied landscape, which stretches from the Pacific Ocean to the Blue Mountains in the northeast. The mountain ranges are very high, with numerous peaks over 9,000 feet, while Hells Canyon, the deepest gorge in the United States, is more than 8,000 feet deep. The western third of the state is mountainous and lush with dense rain forests. The eastern part of the state is characterized by arid deserts. Oregon's coastline is made up largely of steep cliffs. The Columbia is Oregon's major river, and its main tributary is the Snake River.

Rocky bluffs can be found along the Oregon coast.

The coastal regions enjoy a mild climate, with January temperatures ranging from freezing to about 45° F. In July coastal temperatures average 60° F. Away from the coast, without the moderating influence of the ocean, Oregon has warm summers, with average high temperatures mostly in the 80s. In January average temperatures in the east can dip as low as 25° F.

QUICK FACTS

Mount Hood, an old volcano, is the highest point in Oregon, at 11,235 feet. The lowest point is sea level, at the Pacific Ocean.

The Metasequoia, an early relative of the redwood tree, grew in great numbers millions of years ago in Oregon. Fossils of this huge tree have been found in Asia and the United States. In the 1940s botanists found living examples of the tree in Asia and sent seeds to the United States, where the tree again began to grow. It is also referred to as the dawn redwood.

At 1,932 feet, Crater Lake is the deepest lake in the United States and the seventh deepest lake in the world.

Crater Lake National Park, in southwestern Oregon, is known for its incredible views and for the intense blue color of the lake's water.

More than half of the forestland in Oregon is owned by the federal government.

NATURAL RESOURCES

One of Oregon's greatest resources is its high-quality Jory soil, which is named after an early pioneer family. More than 300,000 acres of Jory soil can be found in the rolling hills around the Willamette Valley. These deep, well-drained soils are excellent for agriculture and forestry.

Forests are found throughout the state. In fact, nearly half of Oregon is covered with forests. West of the Cascades most of the trees are Douglas firs. Ponderosa pines are the most common trees east of the Cascades. The abundant forests provided the raw materials for Oregon's first major industry—logging.

Much of Oregon is mountainous. The eastern part of the state and the wide valleys between the mountain ranges, however, provide excellent grasslands for cattle grazing and for the production of wheat, barley, and vegetables.

QUICK FACTS

Almost 80 million seedlings for new trees are planted in Oregon each year.

The Oregon Natural Resources Council helped to create the Endangered American Wilderness Act and the Oregon Wilderness Act, which protect more than 1.2 million acres of land in Oregon.

Gravel, sand, cement, and stone are mined in Oregon.

Jory soil is the unofficial state soil.

Oregon's Jory soil is used for growing crops such as Christmas trees, grass seeds, and wine grapes.

In 1995 Oregon created the nation's first state-sponsored tree program. It is designed to make the public aware of the importance of Oregon's trees.

PLANTS AND ANIMALS

Oregon's landscape is a spectacular combination of forests and vibrant wildflowers such as azaleas and Columbia lilies. Cedars, cottonwoods, firs, hemlocks, maples, pines, and spruces all grow in Oregon's forests.

The state tree is the Douglas fir, which was named after William Douglas, a Scottish botanist who visited the area in 1825. These giant trees average 200 feet in height with a trunk diameter of 6 feet, but they can grow to 325 feet with a 15-foot diameter. The Douglas fir has contributed significantly to Oregon's extensive logging industry.

QUICK FACTS

The state flower is the Oregon grape, which can be found throughout the state.

Oregon's state bird, the western meadowlark, has a beautiful and easily identifiable song.

The state insect is the Oregon swallowtail, a yellow butterfly.

The Oregon Zoo, in Portland, has the country's most successful breeding program for Asian elephants.

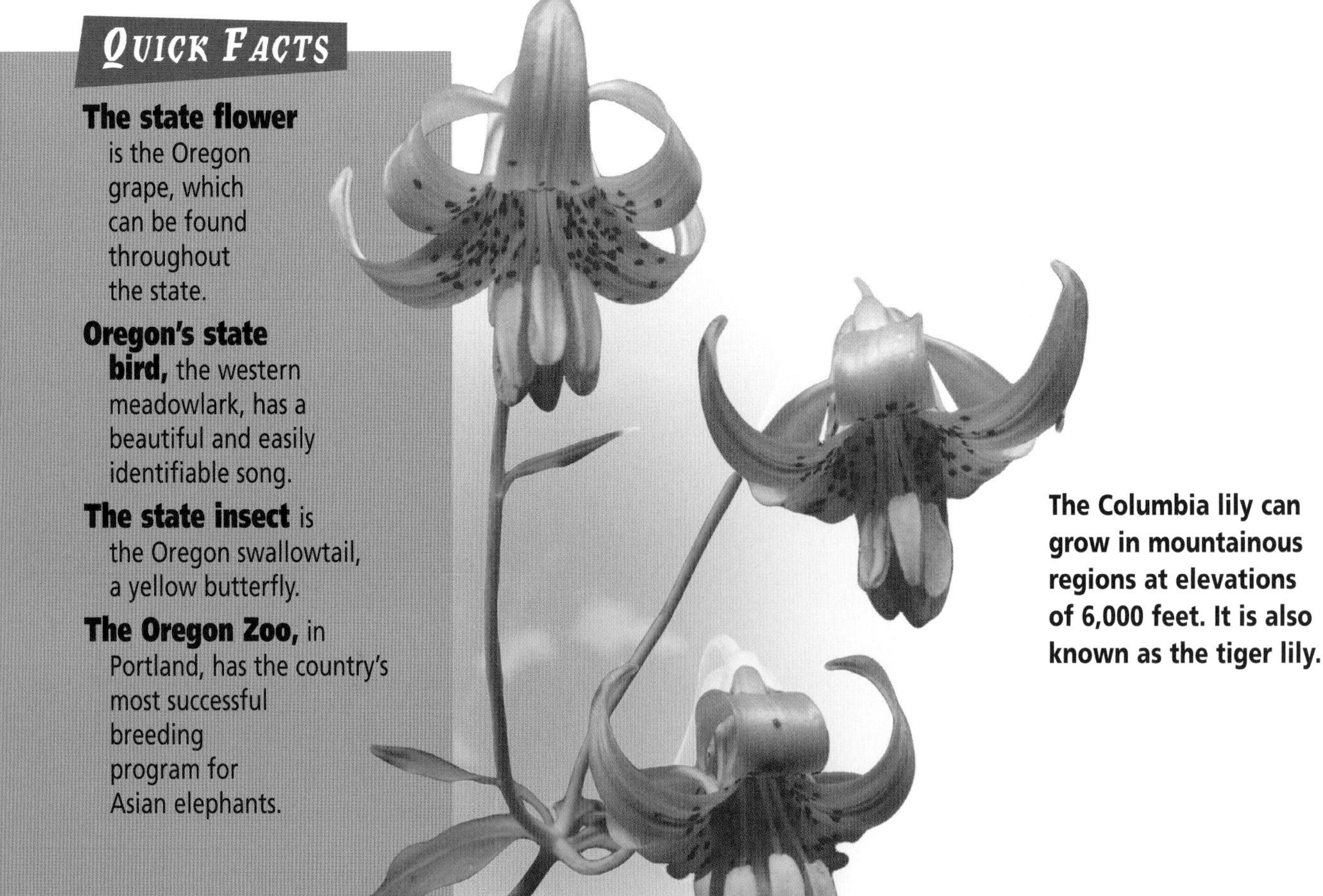

The Columbia lily can grow in mountainous regions at elevations of 6,000 feet. It is also known as the tiger lily.

QUICK FACTS

The state fish is the Chinook salmon. It is the largest of the Pacific salmons and is also known as the spring, king, and tyee salmon.

The Seaside Aquarium, in Seaside, Ore., one of the oldest aquariums on the West coast, was founded in 1937.

Oregon's first wildlife protection laws were developed in the 1890s. The laws were intended to protect the declining populations of beavers, bobcats, cougars, coyotes, and wolves.

Oregon still has a thriving animal population. The state is home to a variety of large animals, including black bears, bighorn sheep, elks, mule deer, pronghorn antelopes, and white-tail deer. Smaller animals are even more numerous. Bobcats, gray and red foxes, martens, muskrats, minks, raccoons, otters, badgers, coyotes, opossums, beavers, and skunks can all be found in Oregon.

Oregon's sea otters were once hunted to near extinction for their fur. They are now being reintroduced to the area.

Oregon's coastal waters are home to sea otters and sea lions. Once numerous, salmon, halibut, and other species of fish are now carefully monitored to protect their numbers. The bull trout has been identified by the U.S. Fish and Wildlife Service as a threatened species in the Columbia River and an endangered species in the Klamath River.

Some 200 elk live in the Jewell Meadows Wildlife Area in Oregon.

Mount Hood offers an exhilarating challenge for climbers.

TOURISM

The mountain ranges, canyons, volcanoes, forests, and coastline of Oregon offer abundant recreational opportunities and attract tourists to the state. Oregonians are careful to balance tourism and environmental protection. The state has nearly 300 miles of protected natural coastline, most of which can be enjoyed by driving along the Pacific Coast Scenic Byway. The route provides travelers with views of beautiful rugged coastline and white sand dunes.

Mountain climbers, rock climbers, and hikers from around the world are drawn to Oregon's numerous mountain ranges. Mount Hood, one of the tallest of the Cascade Mountains, is a popular destination for mountaineers.

Oregon attracts hikers and campers from around the world.

QUICK FACTS

Ranger, a climbing dog that lived from 1925 to 1939, reportedly climbed Mount Hood a total of 500 times in his life. He is buried at the top of the mountain.

The first wedding to be held at the top of Mount Hood was in July 1915.

The Painted Hills, at the John Day Fossil Beds National Monument, are a popular tourist destination. The stripes of color are the result of layers of volcanic ash.

Oregon supplies more saw timber than any other state.

INDUSTRY

Manufacturing accounts for about one fourth of Oregon's **gross state product** and employs about one seventh of the state's workers. The production of forest products such as lumber, plywood, pulp, and paper remains a major industry, though its importance began to decline in the 1980s. To protect animal habitats, shade, and the rain forests, tree harvesting in Oregon is done in an environmentally sensitive manner.

In the 1990s, mostly because of the decline in the forest-products industry, high technology became an increasingly important part of Oregon's economy. High-technology industries include the manufacture of electronics and electrical products, computer software, computer equipment, and **semiconductors**. By the start of the 21st century nearly one fourth of the Oregonians who worked in manufacturing were employed in high-technology industries.

QUICK FACTS

The last nickel mine in the United States, located in Riddle, Ore., closed in 1987.

Food processing, metal manufacturing, and the production of transportation equipment are important to Oregon's economy.

Tektronix, a major electronics firm, was founded in Oregon in 1946.

To reduce pollution, in 1977 Oregon became the first state to enact a law banning aerosol sprays.

Oregon ranks second in the country, after Washington State, in the production of **hydroelectricity.** Hydroelectric plants generate most of the state's electricity.

Operated by the U.S. Army Corps of Engineers, Bonneville Dam, on the Columbia River, has supplied the region with electrical power since 1938.

Agriculture is responsible for about 3 percent of Oregon's gross state product.

GOODS AND SERVICES

Oregon has more than 40,000 farms, which contribute more than $3 billion to the state's economy each year. Oregon is well known for the diversity of its agriculture. The state's different climate zones and rich soils produce a wide variety of crops, including Christmas trees, hazelnuts, peppermint, potatoes, orchard fruits, and wine grapes. Four fifths of Oregon's agricultural products are sold outside of the state, with nearly half going to other countries.

There are more than 3,000 licensed commercial fishermen in Oregon and about 80 species of commercially valuable fish in the state's coastal and inland waters. Shellfish such as oysters, mussels, clams, shrimp, crabs, and scallops are harvested on the coast. Although overfishing has led to a decline in Oregon's salmon fishing industry, salmon is still an important commercial catch.

QUICK FACTS

Oregon produces 99 percent of the hazelnuts grown in the United States.

Farmland covers 17.2 million acres of Oregon's land.

Bill Bowerman, a track coach at the University of Oregon, teamed up with Phil Knight in the 1960s to create Nike Corporation, which grew out of a need for a better running shoe.

Pendleton Woolen Mills is well known for its fine blankets, robes, and shawls.

Salmon are an important catch for both commercial and recreational fishers in Oregon.

Beef cattle are an important livestock product in Oregon.

The service sector plays a dominant role in Oregon's economy, accounting for about three fourths of the jobs in the state. Wholesale and retail firms are among the state's largest employers. Other important service industries include banking, government, real estate, and health and social services.

The first schools in the Oregon region opened in the 1830s. The legislature of the Oregon Territory set up a free public school system in 1849. Oregon has a variety of public and private colleges and universities, including the University of Portland, the University of Oregon (in Eugene), Oregon State University (in Corvallis), Pacific University (in Forest Grove), and Reed College (in Portland).

Oregonians keep current by reading one of the state's many daily newspapers, including the *Oregonian* (Portland), the *Register-Guard* (Eugene), and the *Statesman Journal* (Salem). Oregon also has many television stations and radio stations that serve a broad range of tastes.

QUICK FACTS

Oregon is one of the world's largest producers of grass seeds.

Linus Carl Pauling, a world-renowned chemist, scientist, and political activist, was born in Portland. Pauling attended Oregon Agricultural College, now Oregon State University, in Corvallis. He won the 1954 Nobel Prize for Chemistry and the 1962 Nobel Prize for Peace.

Oregon ranks among the country's leading producers of raspberries, boysenberries, and loganberries.

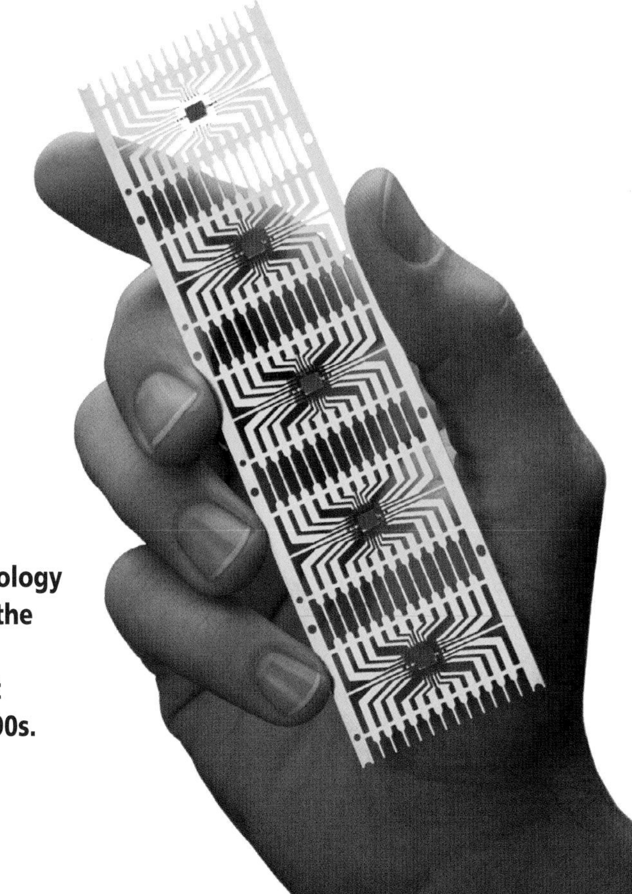

Oregon's high-technology industries began in the 1960s but became especially important beginning in the 1990s.

The Yakima call themselves the Waptailmim, which means "People of the Narrows."

NATIVE AMERICANS

Long before white settlers arrived, an estimated 100,000 to 180,000 Native Americans lived in the Oregon region. When Lewis and Clark arrived in the Oregon area in 1805, they noted in their journals that Oregon was populated by many thousands of Native Americans. The Native Americans who lived in what is now Oregon before the arrival of white settlers belonged to about 125 tribes. Among them were the Chinook, the Nez Perce, the Umatilla, the Paiute, and Klamath and Modoc.

Within only a few decades after contact with the settlers, many of the Native American groups living in the area had been wiped out by disease. The Native Americans had no natural defenses against the diseases brought by the newcomers, which included malaria, chicken pox, measles, and whooping cough. A long series of wars, lasting from 1847 to 1880, also took its toll on the Native American population. By the 1880s most of the state's remaining Native Americans had been moved to reservations.

QUICK FACTS

Many Native Americans in what is now Oregon held potlaches, which were elaborate gift-giving ceremonies that confirmed the social status of both the gift giver and the gift receiver. The more important the host, the bigger the ceremony; the more important the guest, the bigger the gift.

Native Americans in Oregon used fire as an aid in both hunting and agriculture. Fires were set to drive deer together to make them easier to hunt, and fires were also set to clear brush from under nut trees.

Chinook jargon, a language that combined a simplified version of Chinook with other Native American, English, and French terms, allowed Native Americans to communicate with American and British fur traders from California to Alaska.

Many modern place names in Oregon are based on local Chinookan names, including Clackamas, Multnomah, Wasco, Cathlamet, and Clatsop.

The Oregon Trail Interpretive Center, in Baker City, preserves the history and the culture of the Native Americans who once lived along the Oregon Trail.

Captain Robert Gray served in the Continental Navy during the American Revolution.

EXPLORERS AND MISSIONARIES

The area that became Oregon attracted the interest of many different European nations. The Spanish explorer Bartolomé Ferrelo, seeking the **Northwest Passage** as part of an expedition led by Juan Cabrillo, may have sailed the Oregon coastline as early as 1543. Some historians believe that the British explorer Sir Francis Drake sailed along Oregon's coast in 1579. Another Spanish seafarer, Sebastian Vizcaino, may have sighted Oregon in 1603. By the 1700s Russia had begun exploring the area in search of an abundant source of furs.

In 1792 Captain Robert Gray, a trader from the United States, became the first American to sail into the mouth of the Columbia River. He named the river after his ship, *Columbia*. The United States soon claimed the Pacific Northwest based on Gray's exploration of the river.

QUICK FACTS

The first Europeans to see the Oregon coast may have been Spanish sailors of the 1500s.

The British explorer Captain James Cook landed on the Oregon coast but never found the opening to the Columbia River.

In 1790 Captain Robert Gray became the first person from the United States to travel around the world. Two years later he explored the Columbia River.

Christian missionaries went to Oregon in the 1830s. The first to arrive were Catholic priests, who were called "Black Robes."

Fur-trading mogul John Jacob Astor was responsible for the founding of Astoria in 1811.

The Oregon Trail was the most important passage to the West in the mid-1800s.

EARLY SETTLERS

Under the terms of the Louisiana Purchase, the United States acquired a vast amount of territory from France. In May 1804 Meriwether Lewis and William Clark left St. Louis, Mo., to lead an expedition across the lands west of the Mississippi River. They traveled overland across the plains, through the Rocky Mountains, and to the mouth of the Columbia River. In the winter of 1804–05 Lewis and Clark hired the interpreters Toussaint Charbonneau and his wife, Sacagawea. Sacagawea was an important addition to Lewis and Clark's party as she was able to guide them through the land of the Shoshone and in the search for edible fruits and vegetables to supplement their diet.

The expedition nearly ended in the late summer of 1805 when it met bad weather in the Rocky Mountains and ran out of provisions. But the party was saved by Nez Perce Indians, who fed the explorers and helped them on their way through the Rockies. Lewis and Clark established a camp, Fort Clatsop, over the winter of 1805–06 at the site of what is now Seaside, Ore., and finally returned to St. Louis in September 1806.

QUICK FACTS

A replica of Lewis and Clark's 1805 winter camp can be seen at the Fort Clatsop National Memorial.

The Lewis and Clark Expedition covered a total distance of 8,000 miles.

Sacagawea's name means "bird woman" in Shoshone.

Fort Vancouver, across the Columbia River from the site of present-day Portland, was the main supply depot for fur trading in the Pacific Northwest.

Oregon's early settlers are represented by the statue of an "Oregon Pioneer" atop the Capitol in Salem.

The first U.S. settlement in the area was a trading post established in Astoria by John Jacob Astor in 1811. The British captured the trading post during the War of 1812, and Astoria remained under the control of the **Hudson's Bay Company** until 1818. Beginning in the 1830s the area was resettled by settlers from Europe and the United States who traveled the Oregon Trail. Many of these pioneers settled in the Willamette River valley, which remained under British control even though many of its residents wanted it to be part of the United States.

An 1846 treaty with Great Britain established Oregon Country as part of the United States, with the northern boundary at the 49th parallel. Today that parallel (as the northern border of Washington State) forms part of the border between Canada and the United States. In 1848 the U.S. government defined the Oregon Territory as the area from the **Continental Divide** to the coast and from the 49th parallel to the 42nd parallel. When Oregon became a state, in 1859, its present, nearly rectangular boundary was established.

QUICK FACTS

Gold was discovered in the Cascade Mountains in 1858, bringing numerous gold miners and other settlers seeking fortune in Oregon.

Numerous small wars were fought between settlers and Native Americans in the Oregon region for several decades in the 1800s.

Many of Oregon's early settlers grew garden vegetables such as potatoes, cabbage, peas, turnips, onions, parsley, tomatoes, and corn.

Oregon is the 10th largest state in land area, yet it has only a little more than 1 percent of the nation's population.

POPULATION

More than 3.4 million people live in Oregon. Portland is the most populous city, followed by Eugene and Salem. The vast majority of the people live west of the Cascade Mountains.

Compared with the rest of the United States, Oregon has experienced a population boom. In the 1990s the population of Oregon increased by more than 20 percent, whereas the population of the United States as a whole increased by 13 percent. But people in Oregon still have plenty of room compared to the rest of the country. The average number of people per square mile in the nation is just under 80, but in Oregon the average is about 35 people per square mile.

QUICK FACTS

Approximately two thirds of Oregon families own their own homes.

About 86 percent of Oregon's people identified themselves as white in the 2000 U.S. census.

Portland has a population of almost 530,000 people. It is nicknamed the City of Roses for its many beautiful parks.

Portland's population has been projected to reach more than 800,000 by 2025.

Completed in 1875, Portland's Pioneer Courthouse operated as a federal court and post office for 58 years.

POLITICS AND GOVERNMENT

The governor of Oregon serves as head of the executive branch of government and is elected to a four-year term. The legislature is composed of the 60 members of the House of Representatives, each serving a two-year term, and the 30 members of the Senate, each serving a four-year term.

The highest court in Oregon is the Supreme Court, which is made up of seven elected justices who serve six-year terms. Oregon's judicial system has municipal, justice, district, and county courts as well as a court of appeals.

Cities and counties in Oregon can form their own government under a system called home rule. Most have chosen the council form of government headed by either a mayor or city manager. Only seven of Oregon's 36 counties presently have their own system of government.

QUICK FACTS

In the 1840s settlers in the Willamette Valley adopted laws based on those of Iowa.

Some of Oregon's best-known politicians include former U.S. Secretary of the Interior Cecil D. Andrus and U.S. Senator Mark Hatfield.

Oregon was the first state to introduce laws that allow voters to recall politicians if they are not satisfied with their performance.

Oregonians are very conscious of the environment and the need to protect the natural beauty of the state. Oregon is well known for the involvement of its citizens in the protection of the ocean and the land.

Oregon's first two State Capitols were destroyed by fire. The third and most recent Capitol, built in the 1930s, is fireproof.

The Scandinavian Festival, in Junction City, attracts visitors from around the country.

CULTURAL GROUPS

Junction City pays homage each year to the cultures of Denmark, Finland, Norway, Sweden, and Iceland with the Scandinavian Festival. Entertainment, activities, and displays of Old World crafts are part of the celebration. During the four-day festival in August, downtown Junction City is transformed into an old-fashioned Scandinavian town. Popular events include folk dancing and storytelling.

At the Tsalila Festival, the Confederated Tribes of Coos, Siuslaw, and Lower Umpqua honor their heritage with dancing, drumming, traditional crafts, and an alder-smoked salmon dinner. The festival takes place each year along the Umpqua riverfront in Reedsport, Ore., as part of the Umpqua River Festival.

QUICK FACTS

The International Museum of Carousel Arts in Hood River contains an enormous collection of carousel horses and other carousel animals.

Begun in 1950, the nation's oldest crawfish festival is held in Tualatin.

The Junction City Scandinavian Festival has been held every year since 1961.

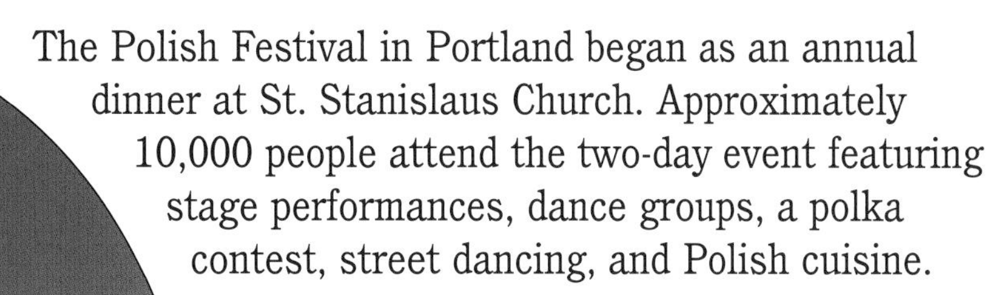

The Polish Festival in Portland began as an annual dinner at St. Stanislaus Church. Approximately 10,000 people attend the two-day event featuring stage performances, dance groups, a polka contest, street dancing, and Polish cuisine.

Oregon's agricultural heritage is celebrated in such events as Sutherlin's Annual Blackberry Festival. It features blackberry cook-offs, craft and food booths, bog races, mud volleyball, and lawn mower races.

The Flock and Fiber Festival, in Canby, celebrates the region's sheep-raising and wool-processing industries. The festival features a sheep show, with top sheep winning prizes in different categories. A variety of wool garments and art is on display throughout the festival.

When Russia sold Alaska to the United States, many Russians who were living there chose to move to Oregon, rather than return to Russia.

QUICK FACTS

Woodburn is home to a community of Russian Old Believers, who split from the Russian Orthodox church in the 1660s.

The first African American to set foot on Oregon soil was Marcus Lopez, a member of Robert Gray's crew.

Portland holds a juggling festival every year.

Portland's Chinatown celebrates the long history of Chinese life in Oregon.

The twin lions at the entrance to Portland's Chinatown are well-known landmarks.

***The Simpsons* is the longest-running prime-time cartoon in television history.**

ARTS AND ENTERTAINMENT

Cultural and artistic life in Oregon is centered around the state's largest cities and fine educational institutions, such as Oregon State University at Corvallis and the University of Oregon at Eugene. Symphony orchestras, ballet and modern dance companies, choirs, and theatrical companies are found in Portland, Eugene, and Salem.

Some major annual entertainment events have contributed greatly to Oregon's reputation in the arts. Perhaps the best known is the Oregon Shakespeare Festival in Ashland. Founded in 1935 as part of Independence Day celebrations, the festival now features one of the most respected Shakespearean troupes in the country. Every year, from February through October, the company performs a selection of plays by Shakespeare and other renowned playwrights.

QUICK FACTS

Matt Groening, creator of *The Simpsons* television show, was born in Portland.

The actress and singer Jane Powell was born in Portland. Powell's roles in Hollywood musicals of the Golden Era earned her the nickname Everyone's Favorite Little Sister.

Oregon's most renowned woman poet, Hazel Hall, was honored with a memorial in 2000 by the Oregon Cultural Heritage Commission. Hall died in 1924 at the age of 38.

The Oregon Country Fair is held annually in July near Eugene. Food and craft booths sell handmade products from across the state.

The Oregon Country Fair began as a school fund-raiser in 1969.

Author Ken Kesey attended the University of Oregon.

The Oregon Coast Music Festival was founded in 1979 as a three-day festival to celebrate the music of the classical composer Joseph Haydn. Since then it has grown into a two-week celebration of everything from classical music to jazz, bluegrass, and world music. Oregon also made its mark on pop music history when a Portland garage band called the Kingsmen had a huge hit with the rock and roll classic "Louie, Louie" in the mid-1960s.

Some of the country's most celebrated authors have come from Oregon. John Reed, the author of *Ten Days That Shook the World*, was born in Portland in 1887. His book was a first-person account of the Russian Revolution of 1917. Many modern journalists have been influenced by his style. Raymond Carver was the author of numerous short stories and collections of poetry. He was born in Clatskanie in 1938. His short stories have been praised as some of the best literature from the United States in the late 20th century. Ken Kesey, the author of *One Flew over the Cuckoo's Nest*, was raised in Oregon.

QUICK FACTS

Doc Severinsen, the longtime bandleader and principal trumpeter for *The Tonight Show* when it was hosted by Johnny Carson, was born in Arlington, Ore.

Filmmaker Gus Van Sant, who directed *Good Will Hunting*, moved to Portland in the 1980s.

Oregon's music festivals include the Oregon Bach Festival, the North by Northwest Music Conference and Festival, the Oregon Festival of American Music, and the Southcoast Dixieland Clambake Jazz Festival.

Sally Struthers, who played the role of Gloria on Norman Lear's groundbreaking television comedy *All in the Family*, was born in Portland.

Ocean fishing is a popular recreational activity in Oregon.

SPORTS

Basketball fans in Oregon follow the Portland Trail Blazers, a National Basketball Association (NBA) team that was formed in 1970. In just seven years the team went from being one of the worst teams in basketball to being one of the best. The Trail Blazers won the NBA championship in the 1976–77 season, creating the phenomenon Oregonians know as "Blazermania." Since then the team has continued to attract large, enthusiastic crowds, first at Memorial Coliseum and then, after 1995, at the Rose Garden.

The Blazers have made many playoff appearances over the years. Top players, such as Clyde Drexler, Kevin Duckworth, Terry Porter, Cliff Robinson, Otis Thorpe, Damon Stoudamire, Brian Grant, and Scottie Pippen, have helped keep Blazermania alive.

QUICK FACTS

The Portland Timbers, the Seattle Sounders, and the Vancouver Whitecaps, rivals in the United Soccer League, compete for a special trophy, the Cascadia Cup.

The Portland Trail Blazers won the NBA championship in 1977.

Oregon's logging history has made lumberjack sports, such as logrolling, very popular.

In Oregon, recreational fishers can fish for salmon, sturgeon, steelhead, walleye, and shad.

In addition to the Blazers, Oregonians enjoy watching the Portland Winter Hawks, a Western Hockey League team that plays in the Rose Quarter complex in Portland, and the Portland Timbers, who play in the United Soccer League. Minor league baseball teams in Oregon include the Portland Beavers, in the Triple-A Pacific Coast League, and the Eugene Emeralds and the Salem-Keizer Volcanoes, in the Single-A Northwest League.

University and college teams enjoy loyal followings as well. The University of Oregon Ducks, the Oregon State Beavers, the Pacific University Boxers, and the Willamette University Bearcats are all outstanding entertainment. Autzen Stadium, home of the Ducks and their dedicated fans, is known to be one of the loudest stadiums in all of college football.

QUICK FACTS

Both Eugene and Portland have been named among the top ten bicycling communities in the country by *Bicycling* magazine.

Dave Kingman, a major league baseball player born in Pendleton, hit 442 home runs during his professional career in the 1970s and 1980s.

Steve Prefontaine was a gifted distance runner whose life was cut short at the age of 24. Two movies were made about him: *Prefontaine* (1997) and *Without Limits* (1998). He is honored every year with a memorial run in his hometown of Coos Bay.

Timberline Lodge Ski Area, at Mount Hood, is the only North American ski resort with year-round skiing.

Dick Fosbury, who was born in Portland and invented the "Fosbury Flop" technique of high jumping, won a gold medal at the 1968 Olympics.

White-water rafting in Oregon is the perfect outdoor adventure.

Brain Teasers

1

How tall are Oregon's tallest trees?

a. about 300 feet

b. about 400 feet

c. about 700 feet

d. about 900 feet

Answer: a. Oregon's tallest trees, Douglas firs, have grown to over 300 feet tall.

2

True or False?

The border between Oregon and California was established in a treaty between the United States and Spain.

Answer: True. The treaty was signed in 1819.

3

True or False?

Oregon is the only state that has an official state nut.

Answer: False. Though the hazelnut is very important to Oregon, several states have official state nuts.

4

The first one-way street was established in Portland in:

a. 1858

b. 1898

c. 1924

d. 1954

Answer: c. The first one-way street in Portland was created in 1924.

5

How tall is Haystack Rock?

a. 102 feet

b. 201 feet

c. 235 feet

d. 325 feet

Answer: c. Haystack Rock is about 235 feet tall.

6

True or False?

Portland was once the capital of Oregon.

Answer: False. Before Salem was chosen as the capital, Oregon City and Corvallis were both territorial state capitals.

7

True or False?

Tillamook Rock Lighthouse is now used as a cemetery.

Answer: True. The lighthouse was turned into a cemetery in 1980.

8

Which city in Oregon has a volcano within its city limits?

Answer: Portland. The city's Mount Tabor Park is home to an extinct volcano.

FACTS AND RESOURCES

About Oregon

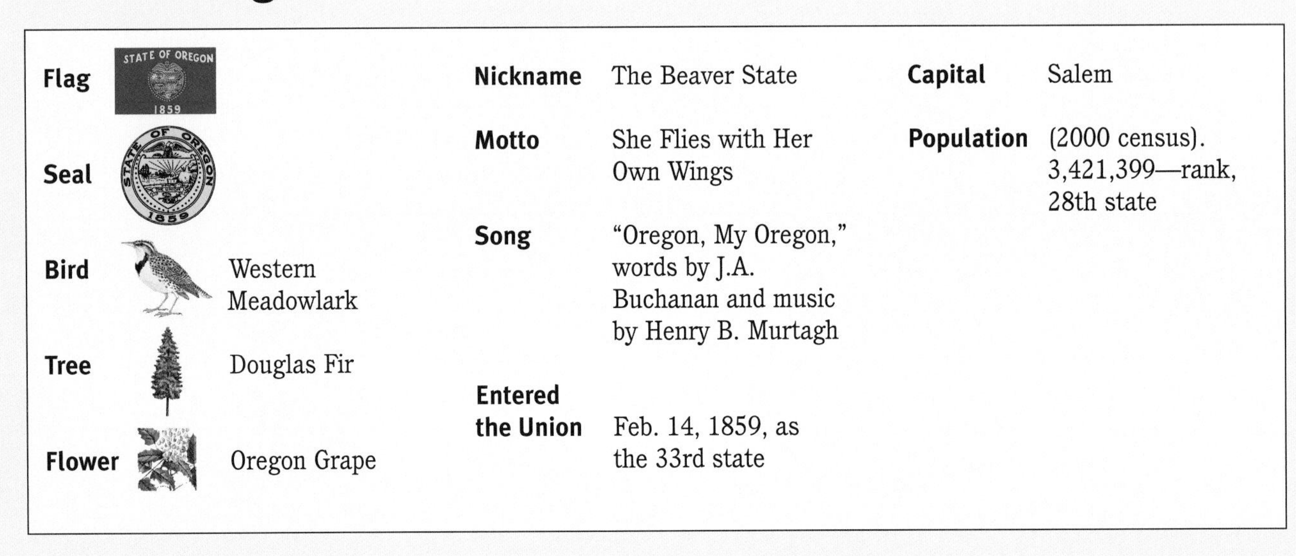

Flag		
Seal		
Bird	Western Meadowlark	
Tree	Douglas Fir	
Flower	Oregon Grape	
Nickname	The Beaver State	
Motto	She Flies with Her Own Wings	
Song	"Oregon, My Oregon," words by J.A. Buchanan and music by Henry B. Murtagh	
Entered the Union	Feb. 14, 1859, as the 33rd state	
Capital	Salem	
Population	(2000 census). 3,421,399—rank, 28th state	

Books

Robbins, William G. *Landscapes of Promise: The Oregon Story, 1800–1940*. Seattle: University of Washington Press, 1997.

Samson, Karl, and Aukshunas, Jane. *Frommer's Oregon,* 3rd ed. New York: Hungry Minds, 2002.

Trinklein, M.J. and Trinklein, Lynne. *Fantastic Facts About the Oregon Trail.* Pocatello, Idaho: Trinklein, 1995.

Web Sites

You can also go online and have a look at the following Web sites:

Oregon OnLine
http://www.state.or.us

Oregon: Just 4 Kids
http://www.econ.state.or.us/kidrptf.htm

The Oregon History Project
http://www.ohs.org/education/oregonhistory/index.cfm

Some Web sites stay current longer than others. To find other Oregon Web sites, enter search terms such as "Oregon," "Portland," "Pacific Northwest," or any other topic you want to research.

GLOSSARY

Continental Divide: an imaginary line along the Rocky Mountains that separates those rivers that flow west to the Pacific Ocean and those that flow east to the Atlantic Ocean

gross state product: the value in dollars of goods and services produced in a state in one year

Hudson's Bay Company: a North American fur-trading company established in 1670

hydroelectricity: energy created from moving water

Louisiana Purchase: a large amount of territory west of the Mississippi River purchased from France by the United States in 1803

migration: a movement of people from one place to another

nickel: a hard, silvery metal used in alloys

Northwest Passage: an ice-free waterway from the Atlantic Ocean to the Pacific Ocean

semiconductors: basic electronic components used in computers and communications equipment

INDEX